Original title:
Evergreen Escapades

Copyright © 2025 Creative Arts Management OÜ
All rights reserved.

Author: Amelia Montgomery
ISBN HARDBACK: 978-1-80566-738-4
ISBN PAPERBACK: 978-1-80566-867-1

Nature's Endless Embrace

In a forest, squirrels dance and prance,
Tree trunks wear hats—a lively chance.
Sunbeams tickle the ferns all day,
While rabbits plot their next grand play.

Birds chirp gossip from limb to limb,
As I slip on moss, lose balance, and swim.
Nature chuckles at my clumsy grace,
Reminds me it's all a joyful race.

A Voyage of Verdant Tides

Leaves shake hands, as breezes toast,
With ladybugs that act like hosts.
I ride a leafboat, just take a chance,
But the wind throws me into a dance!

Frogs burst in laughter, juggling flies,
While turtles yawn and roll their eyes.
"Catch me if you can!" I hear them say,
I trip on roots—oh, the price I pay!

Forest Whispers and Timeless Dances

Beneath the oaks, a secret rave,
Where shadows groove, and light behaves.
Pixies sip tea, gossip in glee,
While I attempt a move, oh, woe is me!

Raccoons wear masks, and start to sway,
Imitating me in the silliest way.
With every stumble, the woodlands cheer,
A clumsy dancer, but have no fear!

Through the Glistening Foliage

Sunlight flickers through the leaves,
Whispers trickle, and laughter weaves.
A deer in shades, sporting a tie,
Dances with rabbits, oh my, oh my!

I grab a branch, take a thrilling leap,
But the bark feels sticky, and I might weep.
Forest spells chuckle, holding me tight,
In this whimsical wood, all feels just right.

A Voyage Along Whispering Trails

We set sail on paths of green,
With squirrels plotting, quite a scene.
A raccoon tried to swipe our map,
But tripped on roots; fell with a clap.

We laughed as we climbed the twisty path,
A bird stole our lunch, oh what a laugh!
Our picnic spread flew with the breeze,
Chasing after it, we fell like leaves.

The trail was winding, a viney maze,
A deer paused to give us a gaze.
We danced around, shouting with glee,
As a turtle raced us—was that a spree?

At dusk, we found our spot to rest,
Under the stars, feeling quite blessed.
But bears! Oh my, they joined the fun,
Stealing our snacks, it's a race we won!

Life in the Tangle of Branches

In the forest where vines do twine,
We found some ants—and wine! Yes, wine!
They marched in unison, dressed in style,
While we just watched, chuckling all the while.

A parrot squawked, gave sage advice,
"Don't sit on logs; they just might slice!"
So off we went, on our merry quest,
With tree trunks laughing, we were their jest.

The owls hooted jokes in the night,
While fireflies danced, oh what a sight!
We slipped on leaves, giggles took flight,
The woods were filled with pure delight.

We built a fort, not quite so tall,
But with laughter echoing, we had it all.
In tangled branches, life is a spree,
Oh, tangled joy, wild and free!

The Luminous Leaf

In a tree with a cheeky grin,
A leaf tried to dance, but fell in.
It laughed at the ground, all covered in dirt,
Said, 'Just a quick break, don't call it a hurt!'

The sun peeked through, with a wink and a tease,
The leaf shouted up, 'Hey, are you pleased?'
To the branches above, it sent a sweet shout,
'Next time I'll bounce; I've got it all figured out!'

Echoing Adventures in Green Silence

In a hollow of trees, where whispers abound,
A raccoon found a hat, oh what a wild sound!
He wore it with flair, like a true forest king,
'This fashion is fierce! Let the critters all sing!'

A squirrel took a leap, in aviator shades,
Said, 'Move over, buddy, I'm making big trades!'
With nuts in his paws and style on his side,
They planned a grand party, with laughter as tide.

Sunbeams on the Forest Floor

Sunbeams tiptoe on leaves like a cat,
Lighting up shadows, as squirrels play pat.
They scamper and chatter, in shades and in light,
While mushrooms get dizzy, what a funny sight!

A turtle moves slow, with a grin full of cheer,
Says, 'Hurry along, my friends, the sun's near!'
But all of his friends were caught in mid-laugh,
Deciding this day was to lounge and do math.

The Playful Gale's Invitation

The wind burst through like a playful young pup,
It tickled the branches and lifted things up.
A hat flew away, and a leaf spun in glee,
Leaving behind all the doubts of a tree!

It called to the flowers, 'Hey, dance with me!'
They twirled and they swayed, with spirited glee.
As petals flew high on this whimsical ride,
Every gust had a giggle, every breeze bravide.

The Essence of Woodland Wonders

In the woods where squirrels talk,
They argue 'bout the best nut stock.
A mushroom sings a silly song,
As rabbits dance all night long.

Trees wear hats made out of leaves,
While ants hold tiny parties, please!
A brook giggles as it flows,
Inviting frogs in fancy clothes.

The sun peeks through a leafy screen,
As chipmunks twirl, a joyful scene.
Acorns fall with a little thud,
And all the creatures celebrate bud!

So join the fun in nature's glee,
Where every critter's wild and free.
With laughter echoing through the air,
The woodland wonders show they care.

Glimpses of the Sacred Grove

In a grove where shadows play,
Unicorns sip tea all day.
They gossip 'bout the latest styles,
And trot around with silly smiles.

A wise old owl cracks silly jokes,
While busy bees don flower pokes.
A hedgehog wears a flowery crown,
As butterflies float all around.

Raccoons in pajamas sing at night,
With fireflies providing light.
They juggle pine cones, oh what a sight!
Creating chaos, pure delight!

Nature's show is quite the scene,
Where nothing is as it might seem.
Join the laughter, feel the groove,
In this magical, funny move!

Echoes of the Earthly Radiance

In the fields where daisies sprout,
A butterfly gets lost, no doubt.
It tries to dance with the bouncing sun,
But twitches its wings, oh what fun!

A duck quacks out the latest news,
While frogs boast of their special blues.
A turtle murmurs with style and grace,
Setting records in a slow pace.

Around the campfire, mice will cheer,
Telling tales that bring you near.
S'mores are missed due to a raid,
Now chocolate fights, oh how they're made!

In the echoes of nature's song,
Join the fun, can't go wrong.
With laughter shared, we'll all ignite,
The radiant joy of pure delight!

The Roam of the Rugged Branches

Branches sway and branches creak,
As squirrels play hide and seek.
They leap and twirl, then tumble down,
With acorns flying all around.

Down below, the grass is thick,
A hedgehog rolls, oh what a trick!
While beetles march in straight, neat rows,
Competing for the best of shows.

The forest floor is full of fun,
As rabbits race and make a run.
They trip on roots, land with a thud,
And start a game of 'who's the stud?'.

With trees that whisper silly tunes,
And sunlight dancing with the moons,
Join the roam, get lost in pleasure,
In nature's laugh, a priceless treasure!

Beneath the Shimmering Canopy

We danced with squirrels, oh what a sight,
The trees were giggling, a comical height.
Branches whispered secrets, all very absurd,
I wondered if trees could actually be heard.

A raccoon wore glasses, quite out of place,
He offered me snacks with a curious grace.
I tripped on a root, just trying to prance,
And laughed as the leaves joined in the dance.

Trails of the Wandering Fern

Along the path where the ferns like to stretch,
I stumbled on rocks, felt my shoe's little sketch.
A snail with a mustache offered me tips,
He said, "Don't rush, take your time for some flips!"

A grasshopper leaped, with style and flair,
He challenged my jump; I fell on a chair.
The forest was laughing, it echoed my plight,
As I rolled in the grass, losing my fight.

A Tapestry of Leaves

In a quilt of leaves, I took my sweet nap,
Awoken by acorns, a funny little slap.
A chipmunk appeared, with a stash oh so grand,
He offered me snacks from his furry little hand.

The colors were bright, like a rainbow gone wild,
With laughter erupting, I felt like a child.
A tree branch tickled me, I jumped with a squeak,
The laughter of nature made my heart leap.

The Music of the Wild

The birds held a concert, but forgot their lines,
A frog played the drums, keeping odd rhymes.
The squirrels were dancing, chasing their tails,
While I tried to sing, but succumbed to my fails.

A bear in a tutu joined in for a song,
While a deer with a bow said, "This can't be wrong!"
We harmonized chaos, a wild serenade,
With giggles and snickers, we all serenade.

Whispers of the Woods

In the woods where the squirrels play,
A raccoon took my sandwich away.
The trees giggle in a breezy dance,
While I trip over roots in a clumsy prance.

Under leaves where shadows creep,
A fox sings songs that make me weep.
The laughter of birds fills up the air,
As branches tickle me without a care.

The mushrooms conspire in colorful plots,
While ants march around, counting their pots.
A deer peeks in, then prances on by,
I swear that I heard it let out a sigh.

With all the giggles that nature displays,
I'll chase my sandwiches in hilarious ways.
In this woodsy world where fun is the law,
I'm just a lost traveler, but I love it raw!

Boundless Canopy Dreams

Up in the trees, a parrot squawks loud,
While a startled owl stands quite unbowed.
The branches twist in a mystical frame,
And squirrels compete to see who can claim.

A raccoon's wearing a shiny old hat,
Flashing a grin as I laugh at the cat.
The sun peeks through with its golden gleam,
Making it hard to tell what's a dream.

With leafy umbrellas above my head,
I dance with the shadows, no need for dread.
While frogs fiddle tunes upon lily pads,
And turtles cheer, shaking their little fads.

In this canopy where giggles abound,
Every twist and turn is joy that I found.
The trees whisper secrets, but I can't quite hear,
That maybe life's best when shared with good cheer!

Secrets Beneath the Pine

Beneath the pine where shadows play,
I discovered an acorn party today.
The dancing bugs boogie without a pause,
While the groundhog critiques with a round of applause.

A snail in a jacket comes strutting by,
Looking for gossip, oh me, oh my!
The roots form a couch, comfy and fine,
As I overhear plans for a moonlit line.

Squirrels gossip while munching on nuts,
Debating if humans wear silly old cuts.
The laughter is loud as the sun starts to fade,
And prancing around are the critters I've made.

Under the boughs, where secrets are spun,
I join in their games, oh, isn't it fun?
With pine scent surrounding and giggles so sweet,
The forest is staging a glorious feat!

Journey Through the Verdant Veil

Through the veil of green, I stumbled and fell,
Chased by a rabbit who rang a small bell.
The ferns were conspirators in leafy disguise,
While I danced through the paths, oh what a surprise!

A badger in spectacles reads from a book,
Telling tall tales that make all of us look.
With every turn comes a giggle or two,
As I dodge the cooing of pigeons in cue.

The sun tickles leaves with a glittery smile,
And the breeze sways my hat – it's gone for a while!
The path winds and bends like a fun twisty slide,
I'm a merry explorer, with nature as guide.

In this journey where laughter leads on,
Every step's a joy, from dusk until dawn.
With friends made of feathers and fur all around,
I'll roam through the veil where the fun knows no bound!

Skyward Gaze Above the Pines

Beneath the tall pines, I lie on the ground,
Watching the squirrels act like they're crowned.
They chatter and scurry, a comical sight,
While I chuckle softly, my heart feels so light.

A raccoon in a hat steals a muffin I dropped,
He dances away, while my laughter won't stop.
With a spider on my nose, I jump like a spring,
Nature's little jesters, oh what joy they bring!

Flourish of the Untamed

In a field of daisies, I trip on my feet,
Amidst the wild blooms, I dance to the beat.
A bee buzzes close, I give him a wave,
He winks back at me, oh what a brave knave!

The grass whispers laughter, tickling my toes,
As I race with a rabbit, who merrily goes.
I tumble and roll, a curious sight,
In the realm of the wild, everything feels right.

Roaming Through Nature's Keep

With a stick as my sword, I venture to fight,
Against imaginary foes in broad daylight.
The trees all around hold their breath in suspense,
While I shout my battle cry, oh so intense!

A chipmunk, my villain, scurries up high,
He mocks my brave quest with a cheeky little sigh.
But I'm resolute, fueled by a quest for a snack,
As I raid my own bag, the victory's back!

The Breath of the Wilderness

In the crisp morning air, I take a big breath,
Misjudging the distance, I nearly meet death.
A branch like a spear jabs straight at my face,
And I wonder if nature's part of the chase.

An owl hoots in laughter, a wise little sage,
As I dance with a fern, like a fool on a stage.
The forest conspires with each comical twist,
In the arms of the wild, how could I resist?

Enchanted Forest Trails

In a forest so dense, where the squirrels wear hats,
I tripped on a root, caused a dance with some rats.
Mushrooms were giggling, some vines tied my shoe,
They whispered, 'Come join us, there's laughter for you!'

The pixies were buzzing, they threw glitter around,
A deer with a bowtie pranced in without sound.
I ducked just in time, as a butterfly flew,
It giggled and swirled, said, 'Catch me if you can too!'

Beneath Canopy Dreams

Beneath leafy arches, I spotted a gnome,
He juggled green apples while shouting, 'I'm home!'
A bear on a unicycle cycled through bramble,
I chuckled so hard, I could barely keep my gamble.

Frogs in sunglasses croaked some tunes for the crowd,
Their jokes were a hit, oh they sang it out loud!
I danced with the trees, doing the twist and the shout,
But a squirrel stole my hat, said, 'You don't need it, out!'

Secrets of the Verdant Realm

In a glade full of secrets, I found a strange brew,
A frog with a top hat offered me a view.
He said, 'Take a sip, but please don't be shy,
You might see the world from very high and dry!'

Tall mushrooms were gossiping, they blushed shades of red,
While otters debated where to nap in their bed.
I slipped on a snail, which was quite a surprise,
He grinned as he sped off, leaving me in the skies!

Journeys in the Green Embrace

Through hedges and thickets, I tripped on a vine,
My shoe flew away while a raccoon sipped wine.
He said with a wink, 'Let's share in the fun,
We'll start a new trend: fashion made on the run!'

Toadstools were dancing, they called me to join,
But my feet were all tangled in very green coin.
I laughed as the sunlight played hide-and-seek,
With shadows that followed, oh what a unique!

Glades of Wonder

In a glade where squirrels dance,
A rabbit tried to take a chance.
He leaped but missed a tasty snack,
And met the ground with quite a thwack.

The trees above all laughed so loud,
As he stood up, embarrassed, bowed.
With fluff and leaves stuck in his fur,
He pondered if he should defer.

A bird swooped down with cheeky glee,
"Try again! Just wobble free!"
The rabbit nodded, tail a wag,
And set off on a funny brag.

In that glade of giggles bright,
Every stumble brought delight.
With friends in nature's silly throng,
The day was silly, joyous, strong.

The Compass of the Canopy

With leaves like sails, the trees conspire,
A compass made of branch and wire.
The raccoon lost his sense of time,
He thought that climbing trees was prime.

Upward he went, all paws a-flail,
His map was scribbled with a trail.
The birds above would squawk and tease,
"Your compass isn't worth a sneeze!"

Adventure calls, he gave a shout,
"Let's find the nuts, give me a route!"
But all the squirrels rolled their eyes,
"Your sense of place is quite a surprise!"

They gathered round, with snacks in tow,
Mapping out a path to go.
In the canopy, their laughter soared,
Who needs a compass when they're adored?

Beneath the Canopy's Embrace

Beneath the leaves, a shadow plays,
A turtle dreams in a slow-paced maze.
Then came a frog with super hops,
"Why move so slow? Just look at the tops!"

The turtle grinned, "I'll take my time,
For life's a journey, not a climb."
While frogs just sprang in leaps and bounds,
The turtle smiled on grassy grounds.

A snail joined in, with wisdom grand,
"Perhaps we all should hold a hand!"
They laughed so much, the sun peeked through,
Who'd think a friendship could grow so true?

In every shade, they found their song,
Beneath the boughs, they danced along.
With giggles shared and tales to share,
Unique in style, a comical pair.

Whispers from the Wilderness

In the woods where whispers tickle leaves,
A porcupine spun tales that deceive.
"Once I raced a fox and a hare,
And lost my quills in a wild affair!"

The fox, it smirked, still agile and sly,
"For you to run, my dear, is a lie!"
They circled 'round, with banter true,
What's a story without a brew?

The owl hooted, "What's all this fuss?
You're all slowpokes, you need a bus!"
Yet the creatures laughed, no rush tonight,
Enjoying the stars in the cool moonlight.

From leaf to leaf, the stories flowed,
As giggles weaved through the forest road.
In the wilderness, where fun ignites,
Every whisper turned into delights.

Tales from the Thicket

In a thicket full of trees,
A squirrel wore a hat with ease,
He held a tea party with a bee,
And offered them both some herbal tea.

The rabbit danced with great delight,
Shoes too big, oh what a sight!
He tripped and fell, not quite so spry,
And laughed so hard, he nearly cried.

The hedgehog spun, a dance so rad,
But spiked shoes made his moves quite bad,
He rolled away, but didn't roam,
For every bush was now his home.

A fox arrived with jokes to share,
He slipped on leaves and madly flared,
With punchlines sharp, he stole the show,
In this thicket, laughter flows.

Shadows of the Ancient Grove

In the grove where shadows play,
An owl hooted night and day,
He gave advice on how to soar,
While perched upon the forest floor.

A raccoon brought a shiny snack,
But tripped and fell—it left a crack,
His friends all laughed, they couldn't stop,
As berries flew from the salad top.

A wise old tree grumbled with glee,
"Who needs to dance? Just sing with me!"
But when he tried to tap his roots,
He wobbled hard and lost his boots.

The mouse in the shadows stole the night,
With tales of cheese and quite a fright,
He squeaked and squealed, but oh what fun,
In this grove, the laughter's never done.

Lush Journeys in Timeless Green

In a land where vines entwine,
A frog claimed he could really shine,
He wore a crown made of daisies,
And croaked out tunes that went all crazy.

A snail decided to join the race,
With a helmet made of a turtle's face,
He inched along, took quite his time,
While cheering birds sang him a rhyme.

A butterfly flapped in a silly fashion,
It danced with flair, pure passion,
But tangled in a web of green,
And cried, "Help me! I can't be seen!"

The journey here is not just grand,
With critters laughing, lending a hand,
In this lush land of constant play,
Every mishap turns to a brighter day.

The Enchanted Trail

On the trail where trouble brews,
A hedgehog wore some funky shoes,
He danced with style, twirling about,
But slipped on moss, and that's no doubt!

A wily fox planned a grand charade,
To fool the critters with tricks he made,
But ended up in a muddy patch,
Losing his pride and quite a scratch.

A parrot perched with quips to share,
Told tales of squirrels who had a flair,
He cracked some jokes, then took a dive,
And landed softly, still alive!

The trail is filled with laughs galore,
Each step a stumble, never a bore,
With every twist and giggle too,
This enchanted trail's for me and you.

Journey to the Heart of Green

In a grove where the laughter hides,
Squirrels play in their silly strides.
They chase each other round the trees,
Whispering secrets in the breeze.

Frogs in toadstools sing their tune,
Underneath a bright, silly moon.
They hop about without a care,
In this dance, nothing's quite fair!

Bumblebees crash like tiny tanks,
Buzzing over flowered pranks.
They'll steal the nectar, what a feat,
Then blame the ants for stealing their beat!

At day's end, the critters rest,
Flat on their backs, feeling blessed.
With chuckles shared under the light,
They dream of mischief, oh what a sight!

Swaying with the Seasons

When spring arrives with flowers spry,
The tulips giggle as they sigh.
The daisies dance, an awkward show,
They trip and tumble; oh no, oh no!

Summer sun makes the bumblebees sweat,
Fanning flowers with a scream, "Not yet!"
But the daisies laugh, so cool and bright,
"Embrace the fun, we'll be alright!"

Autumn leaves begin to fall,
Squirrels gather, having a ball.
With acorns swirling, they spin in glee,
A forest party with quite the spree!

Winter comes with snowflakes white,
The trees wear coats, such a sight!
While they shiver, the birds all joke,
"Let's build a snowman, or at least a bloke!"

Secrets of the Leafy Realm

Deep in the woods where giggles bloom,
Lies a secret without much room.
The fungi giggle, sharing their lore,
Of the fairies dancing and more!

The mushrooms whisper behind trees tall,
"Who's eating what? We see it all!"
With a wink and a hop, they make a plan,
To trick the deer as best they can!

A rabbit's snicker breaks the silence,
As nature's pranks grow in violins.
"Why did the leaf fall?" he slyly teased,
"To make way for jokes, it's always pleased!"

In this leafy extensive hall,
Laughter echoes, a joyous call.
In the realm where mischief does play,
Even the sunshine can't get away!

Paths of Perpetual Bloom

Through winding paths, the flowers tease,
They sway and twirl in the warm breeze.
"Why be serious?" daffodils shout,
"When life is just a silly flout!"

The roses blushing with fragrant pride,
Cackle softly, "Come join the ride!
We've got petals and giggles galore,
Let's paint this garden with laughter more!"

Tulips strategize how to outshine,
Daring buttercups to join the line.
They play games of hide and seek,
While bees buzz loudly in joyful squeaks.

As evening falls and shadows grow,
The flowers giggle at the show.
"Tomorrow's sun brings chance anew,
For more flowers to laugh, oh yes, it's true!"

Adventures in Nature's Embrace

In the woods where trees wear hats,
Squirrels gossip, sharing chats.
I tripped on roots, landed on a leaf,
Laughed so hard, I forgot my grief.

Bumblebees buzzing, doing their dance,
I tried to waltz, but lost my pants.
A raccoon chuckled, showing his teeth,
Nature's got jokes, oh joy beneath!

With every stumble, laughter flows,
Uneven paths where anything goes.
Found a berry, must taste it now,
Turns out, a sour face I'll allow!

Under the sun, with mud on my feet,
I chased my hat, what a silly feat.
Giggles echoed through the tall pines,
These wacky times, where joy aligns.

Bliss in the Boughs

Perched on a branch, I felt so free,
A bird passed by, said, 'What a tree!'
Forgot my snacks, what a shock,
Now I'm munching on a wayward rock.

Sunlight dapples the forest floor,
I chased a shadow, then found a door.
It led to nowhere, just a big tree,
But laughter's the key, it's always a spree!

Mice are giggling, playing their games,
I joined their fun, but no one knew names.
Every flip and fall was pure delight,
Nature's so funny, from morning to night.

With laughter bubbling under the sky,
I spied a raccoon, thought I'd give it a try.
He stole my hat with a cheeky grin,
In this woodland comedy, we all win!

Wandering Through the Verdant Wilds

Lost in the green, with bugs in my hair,
Chasing a deer, but what a scare!
Stumbled upon a snail in a race,
He's slow but steady, perhaps my pace?

Flowers giggled as I passed by,
Their petals swaying, oh my oh my!
A caterpillar whispered, 'What's your plan?'
I just want to eat, oh snack in hand!

Rabbits chuckled, hopping with glee,
I tried to join, but fell on my knee.
With every tumble, the laughter grew,
A day in the wild, so much to pursue!

A quirky fox offered me a seat,
But his jokes were bad, can't take the heat!
Nature's a circus, with merriment grand,
In these woven woods, I'll always stand.

Trails of Tranquil Discovery

On the path, I met a wise old tree,
He said, 'What's up? Just you and me!'
I shared my woes, he just swayed,
Turns out, he's a great listener, I was played.

A chipmunk danced like a little star,
I tried to copy, but fell from afar.
Rolling in laughter, the earth's sweet embrace,
Nature's my stage, and I'm not out of place!

Butterflies fluttered, pull a stunt or two,
I waved my arms, pretending to woo.
They laughed, or so I think, as they flew high,
In this playful realm, oh how time flies!

In the stillness, a frog croaked a tune,
I couldn't help it, I joined the monsoon.
With giggles and grins, we danced in the rain,
This wild adventure, that's never mundane!

Children's Laughter in Green Fields

In fields of green, where giggles ring,
Little feet dance, and flowers sing.
A butterfly wears a silly hat,
While kids chase shadows, imagining a cat.

Kites fly high, with tails like tails,
One gets stuck—oh, how it fails!
They bowl down hills, a raucous sight,
With mud on noses, pure delight!

Picnics with sandwiches strangely shaped,
One's a monster, another's draped.
They laugh at jokes only they know,
As ants join in for an unexpected show.

And when the sun dips lower still,
They plot to catch a firefly thrill.
Childhood bliss in every cheer,
In that green field, laughter is clear.

Twilight in the Timberland

When twilight paints the trees with gold,
The squirrels spin tales, both silly and bold.
A raccoon juggles acorns with flair,
While owls sit pondering who's smarter, beware!

The campfire crackles, stories unfold,
Of a brave rabbit, or so we are told.
A marshmallow fight breaks out with glee,
Sticky fingers on all—oh, what a spree!

Ghosts of timberlan ds, they dance in the breeze,
Spookier still, are the rustling leaves.
Laughter echoes as shadows collide,
The night's filled with jokes the moon cannot hide.

Stars peek through where the branches weave,
Kids tell tall tales, you'd hardly believe.
Twilight whispers, "See what's outside!"
In timberland's embrace, joy cannot hide.

Embrace of the Ever-Blooming

In gardens bright where colors clash,
Bumblebees dance, creating a splash.
A flower sneezes, pollen in the air,
"Bless you!" they giggle, without a care.

The sun winks down, it's a sight to see,
A snail on a mission, plotting to be free.
Chasing butterflies takes a toll,
Yet they all end up in a tangled stroll.

Tulips twitch, as if they can chat,
While daisies giggle, "Check out that cat!"
The gardener trips, oh, what a slap!
They all burst out laughing, what a mishap!

In blooms of joy, the laughter's bright,
Seeds of humor sprout day and night.
In this garden, with giggles, we bloom,
Spreading fun, chasing away gloom.

Serendipity Among the Pines

Among the pines, where laughter spreads,
A raccoon kicks pinecones, fills folks with dreads.
A squirrel steals snacks, it's quite the thrill,
These playful antics could give you a chill!

A picnic set, under branches wide,
They munch on fruits, roasted with pride.
A bird sings loudly, joining the feast,
With rhythm so odd, it's a parody least!

Suddenly a pine cone drops with a thud,
Everyone jumps—was it a bear or just mud?
They laugh at their fears, brush off the pine,
In this woodsy world, it's all quite divine!

As dusk blankets all in a soft embrace,
They dance around fireflies, swaying with grace.
Serendipity reigns, what a merry sight,
In the heart of the pines, all troubles take flight!

The Lush Haven Awaits

In the woods where laughter thrives,
Squirrels dance in jolly dives.
Mushrooms wear a tiny hat,
While gnomes chase a giggling cat.

Berries burst with juicy flair,
Ants parade without a care.
Leaves are laughing, can you hear?
Nature's got a party here!

The brook sings a silly tune,
As frogs croak under the moon.
Rabbits hop, a joyful scene,
While owls plot their mischief keen.

So grab your friends, join the spree,
In this place of jubilee.
Where whimsy paints the sky so bright,
And every day feels just right.

Among the Timeless Trees

Beneath the boughs, the giggles grow,
Where wise old trees put on a show.
A raccoon steals a shiny spoon,
While birds compose a silly tune.

Bark and branches stretch so grand,
Unruly vines make quite the band.
A chipmunk jokes with a pine cone,
Echoes of laughter, like a drone.

Bees in bowties buzz around,
Joking with flowers, so profound.
Morning glories start to chime,
As sunlight dances, oh so prime.

So come and join this lively place,
Where nature wears a smiling face.
With each step, hilarity flows,
In these woods where humor grows.

A Treetop Symphony

Up in the trees, the songbirds play,
Singing of cheese in a funny way.
Raccoons tap dance on the leaves,
While playful squirrels pull up their sleeves.

The branches sway to a wacky beat,
As critters gather for a treat.
An acorn falls, a drumstick thud,
The forest floor's a wiggly flood.

Near the nests, a parrot squawks,
Sharing jokes in flappy talks.
A snail slides in with goofy glee,
Claiming he's as fast as can be.

So take a moment, hear their song,
In the treetops where you belong.
With nature's laugh, your heart will sing,
In this realm of goofy swing.

Echoes of the Mossy Floor

On the ground where soft moss lies,
Frogs tell jokes in silly ties.
A turtle grins, a snail takes a bow,
As laughter fills the air somehow.

The mushrooms giggle in the shade,
Where happy critters have parades.
A beetle spins a wild small dance,
Inviting all for a merry chance.

With shadows dancing on the green,
Each twist and turn feels like a dream.
The whispers of the earth are true,
Filled with fun and joy anew.

So stomp around, don't walk too slow,
Join the party down below.
With every laugh, the world feels bright,
In this playful, leafy light.

Memories Among the Cedars

In the woods where squirrels dance,
I tripped on roots, forgot my pants.
A deer laughed, what a sight,
As I fumbled, trying to take flight.

Beneath the boughs, we played hide-and-seek,
The trees exchanged glances, so to speak.
With sticky sap on my shoe,
I swore I'd never come back to the zoo.

Birds chirped jokes that flew overhead,
While I twirled, landing face down instead.
Giggles echoed through the green,
As I rolled away, trying to stay unseen.

With pinecone hats and acorn gear,
My friends declared it the best year.
Laughter lingered like the scent of pine,
In these woods, everything felt just fine.

Journeying Through Nature's Quilt

Stumbling through a field of blooms,
I tripped on daisies, fell with a boom!
A butterfly giggled, flew away,
While I lay chuckling in the fray.

Patchwork paths of leaves and grass,
I mistook a squirrel for a class.
He scolded me for not being wise,
As I scratched my head, full of surprise.

Tangled vines became my foe,
As I raced the wind, oh what a show!
Nature's laundry hung all around,
And I lost my shirt under a mound.

With every step, my laughter grew,
The trees would sway, chuckle too.
In this vibrant, silly spree,
Nature's quilt felt so carefree.

Treading Softly on Moss-Covered Earth

With every step, a squishy sound,
I thought I'd found a treasure mound.
But what I found was rather sly,
A sleeping frog, not shy to pry.

Mossy slippers made me slip,
As I took a fateful dip.
The ground giggled, oh what fun,
While I made friends with a setting sun.

In this green carpet, I danced around,
Trying to bounce, I touched the ground.
The trees would whisper, 'Watch your back!'
As I landed, in a mossy sack.

Chasing shadows, I leapt with glee,
Thinking the forest was playing with me.
From mushrooms to bugs, all in cheer,
This slippery tale, I hold so dear.

Wandering in the Shadows of Giants

Under towering trees, I peered up high,
Bumped my head, oh my, oh my!
A giant's laughter thundered near,
As I dusted off, confronting my fear.

With tree trunks like castles, oh so stout,
I played a knight, and danced about.
Woodpecker drummed, a rhythmic show,
As I wobbled, and my confidence did grow.

Silly antics, twirls and leaps,
The forest watched while I made heaps.
A raccoon joined in on the fun,
Rolling and laughing 'til day was done.

Amongst these giants, I found my place,
With furry friends, I joined the race.
Nature's humor, bright and free,
These wooded wonders, just like me!

Echoes of the Leafy Labyrinth

In a maze of green, I lose my way,
Chasing squirrels that dance and sway.
The bushes giggle, the branches tease,
As I trip on roots, oh, what a breeze!

Mapping the paths with a paper map,
I find a pond where frogs take a nap.
They croak a tune, I join in delight,
A froggy chorus under the moonlight.

A raccoon peeks from behind a tree,
With wide eyes, it stares straight at me.
I wave my hands, it waves right back,
But then it snickers, I feel a little whack!

Nature's giggles fill the air,
Every shadow seems to dare.
In this leafy maze, so full of fun,
The laughter echoes, we're never done!

Sunlit Strolls Among the Firs

Beneath the tall firs, the sun shines bright,
I dance like a fool, quite a funny sight.
A chipmunk chuckles, my partner in crime,
As we skip and twirl, keeping perfect time.

The bugs join in with a buzzing beat,
I step on a twig; oh, what a feat!
The branches sway like a playful crowd,
I bow to the flowers, feeling so proud.

A sunbeam flickers, it tickles my nose,
I sneeze and tumble... where it goes, who knows!
The firs just giggle, their needles do sway,
As I roll in the grass, what a sunny day!

With laughter echoing far and wide,
In this joyous journey, I take great pride.
A silly stroll, with nature as my guide,
In this playful realm, I can't help but glide!

Adventures in the Emerald Wilderness

In the emerald woods, where the path gets lost,
I bumble and stumble, oh, what a cost!
The ferns laugh loudly, tickling my feet,
While mushrooms wink as I shuffle and greet.

A bear does a jig, it's quite the scene,
I join right in, feeling so keen.
The trees are clapping, their leaves in a whirl,
While I spin around in a dizzying twirl.

With tiny ants marching in perfect parade,
I salute them proudly, but then I invfade.
They just keep marching, unfazed and quite bold,
As I lie on the ground, in the sun, uncontrolled.

This wild adventure, filled with delight,
Where critters romp and everything's bright.
I laugh with the leaves, the forest's my friend,
In this wacky wilderness, the fun never ends!

Beneath the Boughs of Serenity

Under boughs so wide, I seek a cool spot,
Where sunlight dapples and peace hits the lot.
I meet a wise owl who offers a grin,
He quips, 'You've got a bear's belly akin!'

The breeze whispers jokes, tickles my ear,
As I chuckle away, they draw near with cheer.
The flowers burst forth with playful applause,
Even the stones nod, breaking their pause.

Suddenly, a squirrel claims the best seat,
'You're in my sun!' I declare, feeling neat.
He twitches his tail and stares with disdain,
But I just laugh loud, he's quite the campaign!

Beneath these great trees, the laughter's a balm,
In a world so wild, everything's calm.
With a giggle here and a chuckle there,
In the heart of the forest, bliss fills the air!

Infinite Adventures in Green

In a field where the grass grows tall,
A squirrel tried to perform a ball.
He slipped on a nut, fell flat with a thud,
And left behind nothing but a puddle of mud.

A rabbit wore shades, posing for fame,
Boasting a selfie, he thought it a game.
But the wind just laughed, blew his hat off his head,
Now he hops 'round naked, it's quite the spread!

A turtle dressed up for a pop star show,
With a mic made of leaves, ready to go.
But he sang so slow, the audience snoozed,
When they woke up, his ballad was merely confused.

Yet every mishap turned belly laughs round,
In this green paradise, joy knows no bound.
The critters unite with their tales full of cheer,
Creating a saga that we hold so dear.

The Forest's Gentle Call

Once a deer thought to strut with flair,
But tripped on a root—oh, what a scare!
He wobbled and tumbled, a comic display,
Now he's known as the forest's ballet.

A porcupine tried to climb up a tree,
With quills all a-quiver, he shouted, "Look at me!"
He got stuck halfway, like a piñata in green,
Now he spins in the breeze, a prickly machine.

A wise old owl, with spectacles round,
Reads the news of the forest, such gossip he's found.
But he snores through the headlines, awake just for tea,
And the forest's deep chatter is all just for free.

Yet through all the antics, the laughter stays bright,
In this whimsical realm, every day is a sight.
The forest may giggle, tease, sing, and shout,
But it holds all its secrets, with laughter throughout.

The Lure of the Shady Groves

In the shadows where sunlight struggles to creep,
A raccoon found snacks and fell into sleep.
He dreamt of a treasure, a feast from the sky,
But woke to a butterfly—oh me, oh my!

A chipmunk who thought she could play the guitar,
Strummed a sad tune by a rusty old car.
But the notes were so squeaky, the critters all fled,
Now she plays for the bugs, who dance instead.

A wise frog declared a karaoke night,
But confused the lyrics—oh, what a fright!
He croaked out a tune about pizza and pie,
Leaving everyone laughing until they could cry.

But in this strange locale, where silliness rules,
These critters make magic, breaking all the tools.
They may misstep and stumble, but always they shine,
In their shady grove, where the laughter's divine.

Roots Beneath the Sky

Beneath the great oak, where the shadows play,
A worm found a hat that had rolled away.
He wore it with pride, a dapper young gent,
Till it rained on his head—now he's fully bent!

A bold little frog with a joke to tell,
Leapt on a log, and off he fell.
The splash made quite ripples, a jovial scene,
As the fish giggled softly, splattered in green.

A fox donned a cape for a grand masquerade,
But the wind stole the show, left his plans in a spade.
Now he runs with the leaves, caught in the chase,
Chasing his tail, it's an awkward embrace!

Yet laughter resounds 'neath the tall, leafy sky,
With every frolic and frolicsome sigh.
In this land of whimsy, where the silly abide,
Nature's own jesters take joy in their pride.

The Enigma of the Verdant Woods

In the woods where squirrels scheme,
With acorns tossed like ice cream,
Giggling trees hide secrets still,
A raccoon's caper gives a thrill.

Footprints lead to a dancing hare,
Tripping over roots with flair,
A chubby fox with a twinkle to share,
Wobbling like he's lost his pair.

The mushrooms wear their polka dots,
While mushrooms burst in giggly knots,
A gnome in red with a laugh so deep,
Whispers tales that make you leap.

So join the fun, don't hang about,
In playful woods where joy's a shout,
With every step, life's a jolly parade,
In the enigma of the verdant glade.

Chasing Mist in the Glades

Through the fog, a llama grins,
With goggles donned, he surely wins,
A fog machine, or is it real?
Tiptoe close, what's the deal?

Lush ferns wave their leafy hands,
In secret dance, with unknown bands,
Funny creatures puff and puff,
Laughing at games too wild and tough.

A parrot sings a silly tune,
To the glow of a cartoon moon,
While frogs forget to leap and croak,
And giggle on their lilypad cloak.

So onward we chase, with laughter bright,
In glades where mists weave day and night,
With every step, a smile we find,
Chasing mist, we're free and unconfined.

Dreaming Under Boughs of Old

Beneath the leaves, a sloth hangs low,
His dreams of speed, not quite a show,
A riddle wrapped in fuzzy dreams,
His thoughts drift soft as moonlight beams.

The branches sway with tales of lore,
Where owls read jokes some might implore,
With one-liners that hit just right,
As yonder fireflies dance in flight.

A wise old turtle thinks aloud,
While critters form an eager crowd,
"Why rush when napping's so sublime?"
Yet giggles echo, chasing time!

So come, lay back and join the fun,
In dreams where worries come undone,
Under boughs old and wise as gold,
We weave our stories, brave and bold.

A Tangle of Adventures Await

In tangled brambles, laughter rings,
With curious critters plotting things,
A bear who wears a spotted tie,
Queries why the sky is shy.

A case of socks disappeared in fright,
Was it the squirrels or a sneaky night?
The search is on with friends in tow,
In funny capers, off we go!

A raccoon steals a picnic snack,
Balancing fruit upon his back,
He grins and winks, says it's all fair,
"Join the chase if you dare!"

Through laughter and a joyful cheer,
In a world where whimsy is dear,
A tangle of adventures awaits each day,
Where silly moments brighten our play.

The Flora's Secret Whirl

In leafy halls where secrets lay,
The flowers dance both night and day.
A daisy twirled, a rose went spin,
With laughter loud, they all joined in.

The tulips told a knock-knock joke,
While violets laughed, they nearly choked.
A daffodil took a silly bow,
Whispering, "What fun! Let's laugh now!"

Through the Garden of Legends

In gardens where the gnomes reside,
Legends frolic, filled with pride.
The carrots boast of their great height,
While peas claim they're the ones to bite.

A pear tree told of fruit so sweet,
While broccoli danced on tiny feet.
With each tale spun, a giggle shared,
In this garden, all are spared.

The Green Pulse of Adventure

There's a path where the mushrooms glow,
And ladybugs put on a show.
A beetle slipped, oh what a sight!
His friends roared with joy, what pure delight!

The whispering leaves became a choir,
Singing tunes that never tire.
A race between squirrels, quick as a dart,
In this realm, adventure won't part.

Unwritten Tales Beneath the Canopy

Beneath the leaves, stories await,
With squirrels that plan and debate.
A fig tree dreams of the skies so wide,
While wise old oaks offer a guide.

Two raccoons giggle as they skit,
Over ups and downs, they tumble, they flit.
With each rustling leaf, new fun begins,
In untold tales where the laughter spins.

The Heartbeat of Enchanted Walks

With every step, a twig does snap,
A squirrel scolds; it's quite a flap.
The path is winding, laughter flows,
Who knew a stroll could spark such shows?

A gnome appears, with silly hat,
He tells a joke; it's quite the spat.
I trip on roots, but all is fair,
In this nutty world, without a care.

The trees are dancing, swaying wide,
I join the jig, with friends beside.
The sunbeams play, in silly hues,
Wandering feet wear mismatched shoes.

At last, we reach the pond's bright shore,
A frog hops by, we laugh some more.
With every gasp and giggle spree,
These walks are pure, absurdity!

In the Shadow of Ancient Roots

Beneath the boughs where shadows creep,
I found a bunch of mushrooms, heap!
They wore small hats, I swear it's true,
With faces grinning, quite askew.

The trees conspire and whisper low,
About the trolls who steal the show.
They tumble out, toes all a-twirl,
Beware their pranks; oh, what a whirl!

I tried to dance, to join their game,
But tripped on roots and lost my fame.
The laughter echoed through the glen,
"Try again, my friend, do not bend!"

Amongst these giants, tales are spun,
With every chuckle, the day is won.
I'll never tire of this sweet cheer,
In roots and giggles, there's no fear!

The Spirit of the Wandering Breeze

A breeze did dance, with whispers sly,
It carried tales of who knows why.
I chased it down, into a field,
Where daffodils wore crowns, revealed.

The wind giggled, tickling my ear,
"Come closer now, don't you fear!"
You'd think it's nonsense as I prance,
But flowers start to sway and dance.

A butterfly joins, in colors bright,
Spinning and swirling, oh what a sight!
With every laugh, the world does bend,
Is this a race, or just pretend?

So off I go, with spirit light,
Into the gust, pure delight.
And who would have thought, when I did flee,
That nature's laughter is wild and free!

Trails Intertwined with Dreams

Upon the path where shadows roll,
I met a fox, heart full of soul.
He spoke in riddles, twinkled his eye,
"Follow me, and let's fly high!"

We twirled around in circles tight,
Until our giggles took flight.
The sun peeked in, through leafy seams,
And caught us tangled, in funny dreams.

With every step, new friends were found,
A hedgehog in a cap came around.
Together we spun, downhill we raced,
Laughing at the silly, whirling haste!

So join the fun on this crazy trail,
Where whims and wonders never pale.
For every twist, and every turn,
Brings laughter loud, and joy to learn!

Wandering through the Forest's Heart

In the woods, I lost my hat,
A squirrel wears it, fancy that!
He prances proud on a branch so high,
I'll steal it back, oh me, oh my.

The trees all chuckle, roots entwined,
While I chase shadows, a little blind.
A bird sings loudly, "Catch if you can!"
But fails to see my wobbly plan.

In a thicket, I trip and roll,
Clouds of leaves, a leafy goal.
A raccoon snickers, he's seen the fall,
"Next time, look before the crawl!"

Leaving behind my tangled dreams,
I shout in vain, "It's not what it seems!"
The forest giggles, soft and light,
As I wander on through day and night.

Nature's Unfurling Mysteries

The daisies gossip, petals aflutter,
While I dance past, caught in their clutter.
A flower sneezes, the bees start to buzz,
"Get back in line," they say, "That's a must!"

In the underbrush, a mystery stirs,
A rabbit hops by, with a face full of furs.
"Why so serious?" I ask, not a chance,
He winks and hops off, in a bunny-like dance.

The willow weeps, but it's not out of gloom,
It just miscalculated its hairstyle's room.
"Get a trim!" I yell, but it bends with grace,
Ignoring my tips, it's found its own space.

Every twig clicks, every leaf crinkles,
As I twirl around, the laughter crinkles.
Lost in the woods with nature at play,
I might never find my way home today!

The Emerald Oasis

In this patch of green, I sip my tea,
A lizard teases, "Share some with me!"
He's got a grin, with bug-stuffed cheeks,
I chuckle and sip, as he softly squeaks.

A fountain giggles, it bubbles and splashes,
"Last one in is a rotten old gnasher!"
I take a leap, with all of my might,
And water swirls, oh what a sight!

Moss carpets the ground, so lush and so thick,
I tumble and slip, oh that was quick!
The frogs start croaking, a concert ensues,
I join in the fun, forgetting the blues.

Sunlight breaks through the leafy embrace,
Lighting up smiles on every face.
This lush escape is one wild spree,
Where laughter and joy grow like the tallest tree!

Dancing with Nature's Palette

With a twirl and a spin, I dance among hues,
Past reds, and blues, up the greens with the prune!
A butterfly giggles as I step wrong,
"Keep up the beat, or you'll not last long!"

The daisies stand tall, in colorful rows,
Each bloom a partner, who easily grows.
We sway to the rhythm of the wind's soft hum,
While ants march by, with a line just for fun.

A water droplet joins, it splashes my shoe,
"Hey, buddy! Watch out, with a laugh, I flew!"
I splash back, we dance with a gleeful delight,
In this vibrant world where we twirl through the night.

As the sun dips low, I stumble, I glide,
In this party of colors, where dreams can't hide.
Growing with laughter, we spin and we sway,
Nature's grand show, come join in the play!

www.ingramcontent.com/pod-product-compliance
Lightning Source LLC
Chambersburg PA
CBHW072140200426
43209CB00051B/186